Karatesaurus

by Robb Lawrence
illustrated by Tim Parker

★ ★

ISBN 0-590-42308-8

12 11 10 9 8 7 6 5 4 3 2 1   9/8 0 1 2 3 4/9

Printed in the U.S.A.   08
First Scholastic printing, September 1989

SCHOLASTIC INC.
New York Toronto London Auckland Sydney

Poor Karatesaurus!

He had to baby-sit Dave and Dinah, the two wildest Sauruses in the neighborhood.

"Hi, kids," said Karatesaurus.

Dave and Dinah had their own way of saying hi. Dave climbed up on Karatesaurus's shoulders and pounded the top of his head as if it were a drum. Dinah climbed onto his back and yelled, "Giddyap, pony!"

Poor Karatesaurus!

"Keep them quiet," their mother told Karatesaurus. "Don't let them get wild."

That's like trying to stop a hurricane! Or an elephant stampede! Or thunder and lightning!

"I'll try," Karatesaurus said.

Karatesaurus wanted to practice his karate. But how could he practice and still take care of Dave and Dinah?

He had an idea. Maybe they would like to learn karate.

"Would you like me to teach you karate?" he asked.

"YAAAAAY!" they both screamed at the top of their lungs.

"We already know karate," said Dave, as he kicked the living room couch.

"Yes. We already know karate," said Dinah as she did hand chops at their pet dog.

"No, no," cried Karatesaurus. "Stop! That's not real karate! That's just kicking and chopping!"

"Yes, it is karate!" cried Dave and Dinah.

They jumped on each other. They wrestled and fought and screamed.

"Stop! Stop!" cried Karatesaurus. "Real karate is an art."

"So is this!" shouted Dave and Dinah.

Karatesaurus finally got them to stop wrestling.

"Karate takes a long time to learn," he told them. "You need control and discipline."

"What's control?" asked Dave.

"What's discipline?" asked Dinah.

"That means you must teach your mind and your muscles to work together," Karatesaurus said. "You must practice your skills every day."

"That's boring," said Dave.

"That's dull," said Dinah.

"First you must learn perfect muscle control," said Karatesaurus.

"I already have good muscles!" cried Dave. "I'll show you."

He kicked the couch again as hard as he could.

"I do, too!" cried Dinah, and she chopped at the dog again.

"Stop! Stop!" Karatesaurus screamed. After half an hour or so, he got them to stop. "That's not control. You've got to train yourself first."

"That's boring," said Dave.

"That's dull," said Dinah.

"For our first lesson," said Karatesaurus, "let's see how long you can stand perfectly still."

"Easy," they said. They stood perfectly still....

....until Dave sneezed!

Then they began to wrestle again.

"Stop! Please stop!" shouted Karatesaurus.

"What about control? What about discipline?"

"Wrestling is more fun," they said.

"Okay, okay. I give up!" cried Karatesaurus.
"All you want to do is wrestle."

"Yes," yelled Dave and Dinah.

"So go ahead and wrestle," said Karatesaurus.
"Wrestle all day long."

"YAAAAY!" they shouted happily.

"But you can't stop until I say so. Deal?"

"Deal!" they cried.

Dave and Dinah wrestled up the living room and down the living room. Then they wrestled across the living room and over the living room.

They wrestled until they were ready to drop. "Can we quit now?" they asked.

"No," said Karatesaurus. "Keep wrestling."

They wrestled some more. And then some more. "Please — can't we stop now?" they begged.

"No," Karatesaurus said firmly. "Keep going."

Dave and Dinah wrestled until they couldn't wrestle anymore. Then they dropped in a heap on the carpet. They didn't move. They *couldn't* move. They were exhausted! And they fell fast asleep.

Their mother returned home. "Goodness, Karatesaurus!" she cried, seeing her children lying peacefully on the floor. "How did you do it?"

"Nothing to it," Karatesaurus said. "It just took a little control and discipline."

"Well, Karatesaurus, you did such a good job," said their mother, "you'll have to come back and baby-sit for them every week!"